HOW DID THEY BUILD THAT?
TUNNEL

BY VICKY FRANCHINO

?

COMMUNITY · CONNECTIONS

HOW DID THEY BUILD THAT? HOW DID THEY BUILD THAT?

eus bens 20:26-

Published in the United States of America by Cherry Lake Publishing
Ann Arbor, Michigan
www.cherrylakepublishing.com

Content Adviser: Nancy Kristof
Reading Adviser: Cecilia Minden-Cupp, PhD, Literacy Consultant

Photo Credits: Cover and page 1, ©M_ART, used under license from Shutterstock, Inc.; page 5, ©iStockphoto.com/zothen; page 7, ©iStockphoto.com/Weim; page 9, ©iStockphoto.com/ mikeuk; page 11, ©qaphotos.com/Alamy; page 13, ©iStockphoto.com/M_D_A; pages 15 and 19, ©iStockphoto.com/melhi; page 17, ©iStockphoto.com/Captainflash; page 21, ©Mathias Beinling/Alamy

LIBRARY OF CONGRESS CATALOGING-IN-PUBLICATION DATA
Franchino, Vicky.
  How did they build that? Tunnel / by Vicky Franchino.
    p. cm.—(Community connections)
  Includes index.
  ISBN-13: 978-1-60279-484-9
  ISBN-10: 1-60279-484-7
  1. Tunnels—Juvenile literature. I. Title. II. Title: Tunnel. III. Series.
  TA807.F73 2010
  624.1'93—dc22   2008045237

Cherry Lake Publishing would like to acknowledge the work of The Partnership for 21st Century Skills. Please visit *www.21stcenturyskills.org* for more information.

TUNNEL

CONTENTS

HOW DID THEY BUILD THAT?

WHY DO PEOPLE BUILD TUNNELS?

Tunnels are special passages. Some tunnels are used for mining. Tunnels can also help make travel faster and easier. Many tunnels help people travel through mountains or water. They take us under roads, too.

Do you see the lights at the top of this mining tunnel? People who work in tunnels need lights to be able to see.

Tunnels help in crowded places. Does your city have a **subway** system? Underground trains don't have to stop for traffic on the street.

Tunnels also help move products from one place to another. They carry telephone wires and electricity to many buildings.

Subway tunnels help people in crowded cities travel more quickly.

Guess how many tunnels are near your home. Don't forget to count sewers. Also, count tunnels that carry electricity cables. Where do you think these tunnels are? Ask an adult to help you think about where they might be.

7

GETTING READY

Building tunnels takes many steps. A **geologist** drills deep holes. He studies samples of rock and soil.

There are different ways to build a tunnel. Sometimes workers start at both ends. They use **lasers** and computers. These tools help the workers meet in the middle.

Geologists are people who study Earth's crust. They know a lot about rocks and soil.

Explosives can be used if the tunnel will go through hard rock. Long ago, workers sometimes used fire to heat the rock. Then they poured cold water on it. This would crack the rock. After that, they could clear it away.

Another way to clear rock is with a tunnel **boring** machine. This has special teeth that help dig through the rock.

These workers are putting together a tunnel boring machine.

One type of tunnel is a cut-and-cover tunnel. For this, workers dig a **trench**. They cover it with a roof. This completes the tunnel **structure**. This type of tunnel can be on land or in water.

For underwater tunnels, sections of the tunnel are dragged into the water. The pieces of the tunnel are sunk to the bottom. Then they are sealed together.

Some tunnels are made to bury pipes.

MAKING THE WALLS AND CEILING

Some tunnels go through softer rock or dirt. Workers use concrete and steel to keep the tunnel from caving in. Concrete is a mixture of cement, sand, gravel, and water. It dries hard and strong. Steel is strong and flexible. Together they make a sturdy lining for many tunnels.

Some tunnels have wall coverings that help make them waterproof.

Some tunnels have roads or railroad tracks in them. Picture all the materials needed to build a road or railroad. Now, imagine having to bring them deep into the ground!

Some tunnels are built so people can drive through mountains.

LOOK!

The shape of a tunnel is important. Most tunnels have an **arch** or circular shape. Arches are strong shapes. Take a good look the next time you see a tunnel. What shapes do you see?

17

KEEPING PEOPLE SAFE

Building a tunnel can be a dangerous job. Workers cover their ears so they don't hurt their hearing. Fresh air is brought in for them to breathe. Workers also use a tool called a **shield**. It holds the tunnel open while workers build the walls and roof.

Workers use headlamps so they can see underground.

Tunnels must also be safe for the people who use them. Fans and air **ducts** carry away air that builds up inside the tunnel. Ducts also bring in fresh air.

Will you travel through a tunnel anytime soon? Remember all the work it took to build it!

This building holds fans that help keep the air fresh in a tunnel in New York City. The tunnel lets cars drive under the water.

THINK!

Tunnels need alarms and sprinklers in case of fire. What other safety features should tunnels have? Hint: think about special ways to get out during a fire or accident.

21

GLOSSARY

arch (ARCH) a curved structure

boring (BOR-ing) able to make a hole by digging or drilling

ducts (DUHKTSS) tubes that air moves through

explosives (ek-SPLOH-sivz) things that can blow up

geologist (jee-OL-uh-jist) someone who studies Earth's layers of rock and soil

lasers (LAY-zurz) devices that make very strong, narrow beams of light

shield (SHEELD) a special frame that protects workers when digging a tunnel in soft material

structure (STRUHK-chur) something that is built

subway (SUHB-way) an underground system of trains

trench (TRENCH) a long, deep ditch

FIND OUT MORE

BOOKS

Kaner, Etta. *Towers and Tunnels*. Tonawanda, NY: Kids Can Press, Ltd., 2009.

Macken, JoAnn Early. *Digging Tunnels*. Mankato, MN: Capstone Press, 2008.

WEB SITES

Big Apple History—Subways
pbskids.org/bigapplehistory/building/topic20.html
Read about the early days of New York's subway system

PBS—Building Big: Tunnels
www.pbs.org/wgbh/buildingbig/tunnel/index.html
Learn about some of the world's most famous tunnels

INDEX

ABOUT THE AUTHOR

Have you ever entered a tunnel in one country and come out in another? Vicky Franchino has! She used to live in Detroit where she and her husband would use the Detroit-Windsor tunnel to go to Canada. That tunnel is almost a mile long and most of it is under the Detroit River. Today Vicky lives in Madison, Wisconsin, with her husband and three daughters.

24